Jam Session

Kobe Bryant

Terri Dougherty

ABDO Publishing Company

SOUTHERN
OKLAHOMA
Library System
Ardmore, Oklahoma

visit us at
www.abdopub.com

Published by ABDO Publishing Company, 4940 Viking Drive, Suite 622, Edina, Minnesota 55435. Copyright © 2000 by Abdo Consulting Group, Inc. International copyrights reserved in all countries. No part of this book may be reproduced in any form without written permission from the publisher.

Printed in the United States.

Cover and Interior Photo credits: AP Wide World Photos; All-Sport Photos

Edited by Denis Dougherty

Sources: Associated Press; Newsweek; New York Daily News; People Magazine; Sports Illustrated; Sports Illustrated For Kids; Time Magazine; ESPN Magazine; USA Today

Library of Congress Cataloging-in-Publication Data

Dougherty, Terri.
    Kobe Bryant / Terri Dougherty.
        p.   cm. -- (Jam Session)
    Includes index.
      ISBN 1-57765-427-7 (hardcover)
      ISBN 1-57765-429-3 (paperback)
    1. Bryant, Kobe, 1978---Juvenile literature.   2. Basketball players--United States--Biography--Juvenile literature. [1. Bryant, Kobe, 1978- . 2. Basketball players.
    3. Afro-Americans--Biography.] I. Title. II. Series.

    GV884.B794 D68 2000
    796.323'092--dc21
    [B]
                                                                    00-033191

Contents

Kobe to the Rescue

Kobe Bryant had dreamed of this moment his entire life. He had imagined taking big shots in big games thousands of times. He had longed to be the star of stars on the biggest basketball stage in the world. Kobe finally got his big chance in Game 4 of the 2000 NBA Finals against the Indiana Pacers. And he was ready.

Kobe was still bothered by a sprained ankle that had kept him out of the previous game. But the 21-year-old ignored the pain and remained calm and confident. He rescued the Los Angeles Lakers after league MVP Shaquille O'Neal fouled out in overtime.

"This is the game you dream about as you're growing up," Kobe said. "You lose yourself in the moment. You are consumed by the game. I just relaxed like I was playing in the backyard."

Kobe hit three huge shots, two jumpers, and a reverse lay-up putback with 5.9 seconds left that gave the Lakers a 120-117 lead over Indiana. The 120-118 victory at Indianapolis put the Lakers up 3-1 in the best-of-seven series.

Kobe finished with 28 points, including eight in overtime. "That was big-time tonight," Lakers teammate Glen Rice said of Kobe. "That had to be the biggest performance of his career. He stepped up like a veteran. That just goes to show how much he has matured."

A few nights later, on June 19 in Los Angeles, Kobe came through again. He made four consecutive pressure-packed free throws in the final 13 seconds of Game 6. The clutch shooting held off the Pacers 116-111 and gave the Lakers their first NBA title since 1988. He finished with 26 points, 10 rebounds, four assists, two blocks, and only one turnover.

It was a fitting end to a spectacular season for Kobe and the Lakers. Kobe had become a superstar and the Lakers had once again become the league's glamour team.

Kobe Bryant goes in for the slam.

Growing Up in Italy

Kobe uses spectacular jams, intense defense, and a brilliant smile to capture the hearts of fans as he streaks to stardom. When a teammate gives him an alley-oop pass, the crowd's cheers roar like thunder as he flies to the basket, catches the ball, and slams it through the hoop.

Kobe's quickness and jumping ability leave fans in awe. His acrobatic moves freeze defenders. His fierce will to win helps him shut down opposing teams' top players. His smile makes girls' hearts melt.

Kobe was famous before he played his first game in the NBA. He went to the pros right after high school. Everyone wanted to know about the polite young man from Philadelphia who was so awesome on the basketball court.

Kobe isn't the only person in his family to have pro basketball experience. His dad, Joe "Jelly Bean" Bryant, played eight seasons in the NBA, with teams in Philadelphia, San Diego, and Houston.

When Kobe was five, his dad signed a contract with a basketball team in Italy. Kobe, his two older sisters, his mom and dad moved across the ocean to Italy. "It was difficult at first because I couldn't speak Italian," Kobe said. "So my two sisters and I got together after school to teach each other the words we had learned. I was able to speak Italian pretty well within a few months."

The family moved around to different cities in Italy as Joe Bryant played for different teams. The Bryants were usually the only black family in a town, and all the moving around made them very close.

Even when he was only eight years old, Kobe liked to tell other kids how good he was at basketball. He backed up what he said on the court.

"He was always so serious about everything he did as far as sports," said his sister Sharia. "Always so intense. When he was eight and I was 11, we were in the same basketball league. The rest of the kids just wanted to play, and he was like, 'I want to win.'"

Most of his friends liked playing soccer better than basketball, so Kobe often practiced by himself. Even though he's now in the NBA, he still perfects his moves by playing one-on-one against his shadow.

"Know what you want to do, see what you want to do, and go get it," Kobe said.

Florence, Italy, where Kobe spent part of his childhood.

Going Pro

Kobe and his family moved back to the United States in 1992, when Kobe was 14. It was a tough adjustment. "When I first got back to the States, I barely spoke English, so that made me the odd man out from the jump," Kobe said. "Combine that with blacks having their own way of talking, and I really had to learn two languages in order to fit."

Although Kobe's English was poor, everyone understood what he was saying on the basketball court. "Basketball was the common denominator," he said. "On the court, I could communicate."

When he was living in Italy, Kobe wondered how good he would be against kids in the United States. He found out on his first day of middle school. "I'm just eating my lunch and this guy comes up to me. He says, 'I hear you're a pretty good basketball player. Well, to be the man, you have to beat the man,' talking about himself. I looked at him like, yeah, okay. So I played him after school—and I shut him out!" Kobe beamed. "And I got respect right there."

Kobe at his high school in 1996. The basketball phenom had his choice of any college but decided to go straight to the NBA.

Kobe was a star at Lower Merion High School in Ardmore, Pennsylvania. When he was a freshman, he bet his best friend that he would be playing in the NBA right after high school.

Kobe worked hard on his game and led his school to the state championship his senior year. He was a 6-foot-5 star who loved to dunk. He averaged 30.8 points, 12.0 rebounds, 6.5 assists, 4.0 steals, and 3.8 blocked shots per game. He was named National High School Player of the Year.

"His success in basketball had little to do with me or his father," said Kobe's mom, Pam. "He was out there on his own working hard."

Kobe was a solid B student. He was already a celebrity, taking singer Brandy to a high school prom and a movie premiere. He was friends with the members of Boyz II Men. At the end of his senior year, Kobe held a press conference in his high school gym. Photographers, reporters, and television crews crowded the hardwood floor.

Kobe at his press conference to announce he is entering the NBA.

Kobe walked up to the podium and announced his decision. "I've decided to skip college and take my talent to the NBA," he said.

The students filling the gym bleachers erupted in cheers. Kobe was going to make his dream come true, and become the first guard to go from high school to the NBA. "Playing in the NBA has been my dream since I was three," Kobe said.

Kobe easily made the jump from high school to the pros. Here he is playing in his first NBA game.

Joining the Lakers

The Charlotte Hornets chose Kobe as the 13th pick of the draft. He was traded to Los Angeles for the Lakers' starting center, Vlade Divac. When Kobe arrived at the Los Angeles airport, someone asked him where he played basketball. "I'm used to saying Lower Merion High School. And then I realized you know, now I'm a Los Angeles Laker. That brought a real big smile to my face," Kobe said. "I'm very excited to be here."

"It's a dream come true to play in the NBA and to come to a team like L.A. that has a great history. Great players like Magic Johnson and Kareem Abdul-Jabbar. It was a team I looked up to when I was growing up."

Kobe was confident he'd do well against players with much more experience. He also realized he had a lot to learn. "I'd be lying if I said I was going into the NBA and didn't think I could make it. If I thought that, I wouldn't be here," he said, adding that he was ready to do whatever the Lakers wanted.

"Wave a towel, hand someone a cup of water, hit a game-winning basket, whatever," he said. "You can expect a hard worker. I will play all out. I've always tried to take bits and pieces of every great player's game into mine, from Kareem's sky hook to James Worthy's jumper."

Kobe's attitude and ability impressed the Lakers. "Guys he has played against will tell you his talent is not 17 years old," said Jerry West, the Lakers general manager. "He was the most-skilled player we've ever worked out, the kind of skill you don't see very often. Five or six years from now, people in L.A. will be talking about him in the highest of terms," said West, who was one of the best guards in NBA history during his playing days in Los Angeles.

Kobe delighted the Los Angeles Lakers fans even in his rookie season.

Kobe moved into a six-bedroom mansion in Pacific Palisades with his parents and one of his sisters. "I'm really happy that my parents will be moving out with me," Kobe said. "We're a close family and we've been together so long—living in Italy and other places—I would have definitely missed the support. "The backbone is the family—once you have that, then everything else is cool. Whether you score 50 points or 0, your family is going to be there."

Kobe's first year with the Lakers wasn't easy. Some people said he shouldn't have skipped college, and others said he shouldn't have been traded to the Lakers. Kobe's rookie season ended on a sour note. In the final seconds of a playoff game against Utah, he launched an air ball from 14 feet that would have won the game. The Lakers lost, ending their season in the second round of the playoffs, but Kobe looked at it as a learning experience.

"It ended with me having to take a long look at my game and what I needed to improve it," Kobe said.

Kobe works on his free throws during a practice session.

Kobe is Fan-tastic

NBA fans embraced Kobe the next season. Even though he wasn't starting for the Lakers, he was named a starter in the All-Star Game at New York. "I'm not really sure why the crowd is so for me other than I'm like the underdog," Kobe said. "People like to see people succeed against the odds."

At 19, Kobe was the youngest all-star in history. He was nervous before the tip-off, but the first time he got the ball he went straight to the hoop for his first of 16 shots—even though he was guarded by basketball legend Michael Jordan. "Had to," Kobe said. "Or he (Jordan) would have killed me. The only thing he understands is aggressiveness."

Kobe scored a team-high 18 points, but his West team lost to the East 135-114. He played 22 minutes, grabbed six rebounds, and had one assist. As he left the Madison Square Garden floor, Michael Jordan took him aside to give him some advice. "I just hugged him and told him to keep going and stay strong because there are always expectations and pressures," Michael said. "I know what too much pressure too soon can do to you and just wanted him to be aware. But he's a smart kid with a bright future. He'll figure it out."

It was a tiring season for Kobe. At times he didn't look like he was having any fun on the court. People said he was "the next Michael Jordan," which was tough to live up to. "The kid is real good and I see a lot of myself in him, no doubt about that," Michael said. "But he's got to be Kobe Bryant and no one else."

Against the New York Knicks, Kobe missed a reverse dunk in the final seconds. The Lakers lost, and some fans said Kobe was more interested in showing off than winning.

"I take this game seriously," he said in his defense. "People act as though I sit on the bench thinking of new ways to dunk and floss (show off). It's not like that. I just love to play the game and it comes through."

Kobe didn't bow to peer pressure. He didn't pierce his ear or get a tatoo.   He wore his hair in an afro, and hung out in mall food courts when the team was on the road. "My parents raised me to be an individual," he said.

In the final game of the regular season, Kobe hit a three-pointer that sealed a win over the Jazz. Three weeks later, the Jazz swept the Lakers in the Western Conference finals. Kobe never lost his positive attitude. After game three, a reporter asked if the Lakers could win the series. Kobe flashed a huge, confident grin and said, "Yeah, I do."

Confident Kobe

*I*n the first round of the 1999 playoffs, Kobe had a chance to show how much he had matured. Far from the rookie struggling to fit in, who hoisted up a season-ending air ball, he had become a confident, all-star performer. He proved it by calmly connecting on two free throws that lifted the Lakers to a victory over Houston.

"I made those free throws at the end of the game and we won," Kobe said. "I've dreamed about that many times."

Kobe scored almost 20 points per game in the 1998-99 season, and averaged 5.3 rebounds and 3.8 assists. "If you really look at my numbers, they're pretty good. And no one is thinking about how I really just got into the game, that I'm still learning and I'm going to make mistakes," Kobe said.

Los Angeles Lakers' Kobe Bryant hangs on the basket after a dunk.

"I don't think anyone can teach the desire and fire he has for the game," teammate Derek Fisher said. "He has the talk, he has the air of confidence about himself—nothing is impossible for him. Even if he goes 3 for 12 one night, he believes he can go 10 for 12 tonight."

Kobe was on the all-star team again, and the chants of the fans made the Lakers move him into the starting lineup. He was in the spotlight in Los Angeles, under everyone's gaze, and was expected to deliver every time he stepped on the court.

"There are times when I go home and think the Lord has given me a lot to deal with," he said. "But I always come to the conclusion that He would never put more of a burden on a person's shoulders than he is ready to bear."

"Everybody here —Magic, Jerry West—they share their knowledge with you. So it was definitely worth it. And I knew since I first came out here for the tryout that it would be all about knowledge."

In the second round of the playoffs, Kobe scored 28 points in a game against San Antonio. However, he missed two crucial free throws and the Spurs won in the final seconds. Kobe grinned sheepishly.

"We've been through so much this year, I think it would be kind of an odd feeling if it wasn't an uphill battle," he said. The Lakers were unable to climb the hill, however, as the Spurs swept the series.

Kobe and Shaq

*E*verything fell into place for the Lakers in the 1999-2000 season. Shaquille O'Neal, the Lakers' veteran superstar center, won the league's MVP award. Even though Shaq was the Lakers' first option on offense, Kobe averaged nearly 23 points per game and again started in the all-star game.

Kobe missed the first 15 games of the season with a fracture in his right hand. But, when he returned, he played with passion as "The Lake Show" stormed to the NBA's best record, finishing their incredible regular season 67-15.

Kobe became a complete player in the 1999-2000 season. Always a talented and exciting offensive player, Kobe also became a defensive star. Kobe's quickness, jumping ability, and desire enabled him to frustrate some of the top scorers in the NBA. For his efforts, Kobe was named to the NBA all-defensive first team.

"I think Kobe's getting a name for himself," said Phil Jackson, who coached the Chicago Bulls to six NBA Championships and took over the Lakers for the 1999-2000 season.

Kobe and Shaq hadn't been the best of friends in previous seasons, but in 1999-2000 they bonded. After a 90-89 win over the Sacramento Kings, Shaq threw the ball into the stands and hugged Kobe in celebration.

In the first round of the playoffs the Lakers outlasted the Kings in a hard fought five game series. Kobe averaged a series high 30.5 points. In the second round, against the Phoenix Suns, Kobe hit a game-winning jump shot in Game 2. The win put the Lakers up 2-0, and they cruised to a 4-1 series victory.

The Western Conference Finals against Portland matched the NBA's top two teams of the regular season. The Lakers grabbed a 3-1 series lead and looked headed for the NBA Finals. Then in Game 5, Kobe sprained his right foot and the Lakers lost. In Game 6, Kobe came back to score 33 points, despite the injury, but the Lakers still lost 103-93.

In the deciding Game 7, the Lakers trailed by 16 points late in the third quarter. It looked like the Lakers' dream season would end in a nightmare. Los Angeles entered the fourth quarter trailing by 13, but suddenly rallied thanks to Kobe. He quickly made two free throws and a jumper. He then threw a perfect lob pass to O'Neal for a dunk. The Lakers won 89-84, and Kobe was the star of the game. He had 25 points, 11 rebounds, seven assists, and four blocks.

In the NBA Finals, the Lakers captured the Championship and concluded their wonderful dream season.

Kobe was also making moves off the court. He recorded a rap album, acted in some commercials, and bought part of a professional basketball team in Italy.

"That (Italy) is my home. That's where I developed a lot of my love for the game. This is something I've always wanted to do, and it's just great that it has happened," Kobe said. "I've always wanted to raise my family in Italy. When my NBA career is over, hopefully I'll be there."

Kobe's family may be starting sometime soon. On May 18, he announced he was engaged to be married to Vanessa Laine. But don't look for Kobe to move to Italy anytime soon. Kobe's NBA career is far from over. His sparkling personality and flair on the court are taking him to the top of the game.

Los Angeles Lakers' Kobe Bryant, left, and Shaquille O'Neal pose for a photo.

Los Angeles Lakers coach
Phil Jackson, right, gives
Kobe instructions during
a break in a game.

Kobe Bryant Profile

Born: August 23, 1978

Height: 6-foot-7

Weight: 210 pounds

Position: Guard

Number: 8

Residence: Pacific Palisades, California

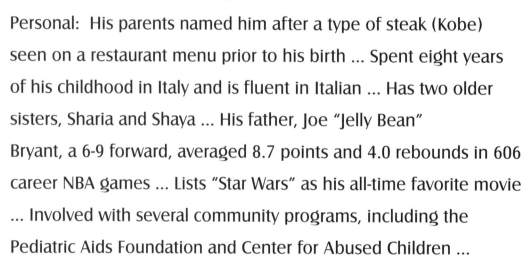

Personal: His parents named him after a type of steak (Kobe) seen on a restaurant menu prior to his birth ... Spent eight years of his childhood in Italy and is fluent in Italian ... Has two older sisters, Sharia and Shaya ... His father, Joe "Jelly Bean" Bryant, a 6-9 forward, averaged 8.7 points and 4.0 rebounds in 606 career NBA games ... Lists "Star Wars" as his all-time favorite movie ... Involved with several community programs, including the Pediatric Aids Foundation and Center for Abused Children ...

Enjoys reading and playing video games ... Says Michael Jordan is the greatest player he has ever seen ... Favorite sports team is the Dallas Cowboys.

Honors

Selected as the National High School Player of the Year as a senior at Lower Merion High School in Ardmore, Pennsylvania (1996) by USA Today and Parade Magazine. Also winner of the Gatorade Circle of Champions and Naismith awards as the nation's top high school player.

Concluded high school career as the all-time leading scorer (2,883 points) in Southeastern Pennsylvania history, surpassing the marks of NBA legend Wilt Chamberlain (2,359) and Carlin Warley (2,441).

Won the slam-dunk competition during the 1997 NBA All-Star Weekend in Cleveland and participated in the Schick Rookie Game, scoring a rookie game record 31 points with eight rebounds.

Named to the 1996-97 NBA All-Rookie second team, becoming the youngest player ever to earn that honor.

Named to the 1998-99 All-NBA third team.

Named to the 1999-2000 All-NBA second team.

Selected to the 1999-2000 NBA all-defensive first team.

Named the NBA player of the week April 10 to April 16, 2000, averaging 29.7 points, seven assists, and six rebounds per game.

Chronology

August 23, 1978 - Kobe Bryant is born in Philadelphia.

1996 - Selected as the National High School Player of the Year as a senior at Lower Merion High School in Ardmore, Pennsylvania.

1996 - Announces he will skip college and go directly from high school to the NBA.

June 26, 1996 - Selected by the Charlotte Hornets with the 13th overall pick in the NBA Draft.

July 11, 1996 - Acquired by the Los Angeles Lakers from the Hornets in exchange for Vlade Divac.

July 24, 1996 - Signs a contract with the Lakers.

November 3, 1996 - Makes his NBA debut at the age of 18 years, two months, and 11 days, against Minnesota.

January 28, 1997 - Becomes the youngest player ever to start an NBA game, scoring 12 points against Dallas.

1997 - Named to the 1996-97 NBA All-Rookie second team, becoming the youngest player ever to earn that honor, after averaging 7.6 points and 15.5 minutes in 71 games.

1998 - Teams with Lisa Leslie of the WNBA's Los Angeles Sparks in the inaugural Nestle Crunch All-Star 2ball competition during All-Star Saturday.

1998 - Becomes the youngest All-Star starter in NBA history, scoring a Western Conference team-high 18 points with six rebounds in the NBA All-Star Game in New York.

1998 - Finishes season as the highest-scoring non-starter in the NBA (15.4 ppg) and the highest-scoring reserve in Los Angeles franchise history (fewer than 10 starts).

1999 - Starts in NBA All-Star Game and scores 15 points.

January 10, 2000 - Scores 27 points in the first half against Denver.

2000 - Starts in NBA All-Star Game and scores 15 points.

March 12, 2000 - Scores a career-high 40 points to go along with 10 rebounds and eight assists in a 109-106 win over Sacramento.

Los Angeles Lakers' Kobe Bryant gestures to the crowd.

Kobe's Stats

Kobe Bryant's regular-season stats with the Los Angeles Lakers

Season	MPG	FG%	3P%	FT%	RPG.	APG.	SPG.	BPG.	PPG
1996-97	15.5	.417	.375	.819	1.9	1.3	.69	.32	7.6
1997-98	26.0	.428	.341	.794	3.1	2.5	.94	.51	15.4
1998-99	37.9	.465	.267	.839	5.3	3.8	1.44	1.0	19.9
1999-00	38.2	.468	.319	.821	6.3	4.9	1.61	.94	22.5

Kobe Bryant's playoff stats with the Los Angeles Lakers

Years	MPG	FG%	3P%	FT%	RPG.	APG.	SPG.	BPG.	PPG
1997-00	30.5	.430	.315	.763	3.7	3.2	1.06	.83	15.9

KEY:

MPG - Minutes per game

FG% - Field-goal percentage

3P% -Three-point field-goal percentage

FT% - Free-throw percentage

RPG - Rebounds per game

APG - Assists per game

SPG - Steals per game

BPG - Blocked shots per game

PPG - Points per game

Kobe at a victory celebration after the Lakers won the NBA Championship.

Kobe's Personal Bests

Points - 40, vs. Sacramento, March 12, 2000

Three-point field goals made - Five, vs. Seattle, January 8, 2000

Assists - 12, vs. Minnesota, December 17, 1999

Steals - 6, vs. Sacramento, April 7, 1999

Rebounds - 14, three times

Blocked shots - 5, twice

Kobe, creating in the air.

Glossary

AIR BALL - To shoot a basketball that doesn't touch the net, rim, or backboard.

ASSIST - A pass to a teammate that leads directly to a basket.

CONFERENCE - A group of athletic teams that compete against each other for a championship.

DEFENSE - Trying to stop the opposing team from scoring.

DRAFT - The process by which professional sports teams choose new players.

DUNK - To slam a ball through the basket.

FREE THROW - To shoot a ball from behind the foul line without being guarded. A player is awarded free throws after being fouled by another player.

GUARD - A basketball player who brings the ball up the court and begins the plays. Teams usually have two guards on the floor.

National Basketball Association (NBA) - A group of teams competing at the highest level of professional basketball.

OFFENSE - The team on the court that has the ball and is trying to score points.

PLAYOFFS - Games played after the regular season to determine the league champion.

STARTER - A player who is on the court when the game begins.

TRADE - A team sends one or more of its players to another team for one or more of its players.

Kobe going in for the reverse lay-up.

Index